OVERCOMING PERFECTIONISM, ANXIETY, AND INDECISION

The Workbook for older Teens and Adults

*Brilliant but Imperfect Exercises
to Release Your Inner Achiever*

CROSS BORDER BOOKS

Table of Contents

Introduction

Perfectionism… The constant need to be flawless, the drive to do tasks perfectly, avoid doing them at all, or simply feel totally dissatisfied, even if you have achieved success.

It's draining; it's counterproductive, and, to be honest, it's downright exhausting most days.

What is the worst thing about perfectionism?

It doesn't set us apart from others, does it?

I mean, study after study shows that perfectionists don't necessarily outperform non-perfectionists, yet here we are… striving for the impossible and failing miserably because the impossible is just that – not possible.

We live on this spinning globe called Earth, where time and the expectations of what we do with our time are just remarkable:

- Work faster
- Work harder
- Work longer
- Work more efficiently
- Be great
- Be wealthy
- Be and do more, more, more!

It can sometimes feel like a never-ending tug-of-war, being pushed, and pulled into becoming something humans are not.

Ultimately, we, as people, are flawed.

Our very design is to fail so that we can learn from the mistakes we make and improve as we move through this journey called life.

We enter this world helpless, and through a series of biological, physiological, and psychological processes, we learn how to function and achieve success.

We stumble, fall, explore, and grow through all of the experiences of our young lives because of our tenacity and our insatiable thirst for exploring the unknown.

So where does it all go wrong?

Why do some of us become stuck in this rut of needing to be perfect?

For most of us, perfectionism rears its head in late childhood before we enter adolescence, when our drive to learn and explore is overtaken by our need to be accepted.

Instead of simply getting up and dusting ourselves off when we make a mistake, we feel embarrassment and shame and associate mistakes with some perceived fatal flaw… (Here's a hint: Mistakes are neither a flaw nor fatal most of the time).

For many years, I went through life proudly proclaiming that I was a perfectionist.

If something didn't feel right or I perceived it to be out of place in my environment, I quickly got to work fixing it, whatever "it" was. My perfectionism was a reflex, and I hid behind it, labeling it *high standards*.

Don't get me wrong. I wasn't oblivious to my high standards; I was just as hard on myself as I was on other people. I wanted to do well in life, and I wanted the same for the people I cared about!

But there was a catch to this impossibly high standard I kept myself to; it was mostly all talk, and I actually didn't get very much done.

I worked on projects for weeks, months, and if you have read *Overcoming Perfectionism, Anxiety, and Indecision*, you'll know it took me even years to complete.

A lot of what I took on was perpetually in the "not done yet" phase because it just wasn't perfect.

I ended up abandoning a lot of these projects because, at some point, I realized that what I envisioned in my mind could never come to fruition.

I'd beat myself up about yet another failure for a couple of weeks, months, or years, and the cycle would repeat… Years of my life went into ideas, planning, preparations, and tinkering without ever reaching an outcome.

Perfectionism had me in its grip, and even though I knew that not all perfectionism is created equal, I was kind of stuck in the toxicity of wanting to be an overachiever.

The irony was, of course, that in my striving for perfection, I wasn't achieving anything at all.

That was until the day of my painting incident and the small steps I took consistently to reclaim myself and pull myself out of the grips of perfectionism.

One of the biggest lessons I learned as I deliriously slapped paint on my boundary wall and as I stumbled my way through other tasks I had never finished was that I couldn't rid myself of perfectionism… And neither can you.

Instead, you need to reframe it and reorient yourself toward what perfection actually is.

Perfect isn't the outcome; it's what you do while striving for an outcome, but the outcome needs to come, whether it's a good one or a pile of glued-together matchsticks that were supposed to be a six-story mini mansion complete with opening shutters and a sprawling front porch.

You can strive for efficiency, greatness, and even quality – heck! You can even strive for perfection, as long as you understand that perfection itself is never going to be the outcome.

The irony is that perfectionism is imperfect.

It's a flawed notion that human beings could ever be perfect while denying the fact that our flaws make us exactly that – *perfect*!

This brings us to the burning question… *How do you Calm the Chaos?*

The answer to that question is complex, multi-faceted, and sometimes fun, just like the techniques, exercises, and tools I have laid out for you in this book.

You will notice as you work through this notebook that I haven't stuck to any one technique because no one technique is foolproof when it comes to perfectionism… Ah, the irony once more.

"But if they're not perfect, how will they work?" I hear you cry!

Well, that's the beauty of freeing yourself from perfectionism – it's the process.

It's finding what works for you, working through the processes, trying, failing, and trying some more.

It's discovering or rediscovering yourself, and what flaws make you imperfectly perfect so that you can *outsmart perfectionism* and reclaim your life.

CHAPTER 1:

Indecisiveness and Perfectionism – Breaking the Ties That Bind Us

Perfectionism may seem superficial to those who view it from the outside.

To others, perfectionism can seem like hard work, diligence, or even self-critical achievement at any expense.

None of this sounds particularly bad, and certainly, those who see a perfectionist don't associate perfectionist tendencies with anything negative.

In the past, I've heard people describe me as "uptight but a really nice guy," and it stung.

I wasn't uptight; I was striving for perfection!

But then, as I continued to take my strides to perfection and as more and more tasks dropped to the wayside and as burnout knocked persistently somewhere in the distance, that narrative changed.

"I don't know what happened to him… He used to be so diligent, but now he just procrastinates everything."

Ouch!

As terrible as it was to hear, the statement was kind of true.

I mean, I had unopened mail dating back a couple of months, that outdoor bench that threatened to collapse every time I sat on it, which I had to fix, a couple of unwritten books, and the now-dead plants I bought six months ago to remind me of all the tasks I had yet to complete.

As I sat – and nearly fell off the bench in my garden – sipping my morning coffee, my eye caught the empty pots that used to house the plants that would become my urban oasis. I agonized for weeks about the *right* spot for them, drawing, redrawing, measuring, and mock-placing each piece of greenery, only to return the pots to their starting point at the end of every planting session.

My inner critic, not missing the chance to make its opinion heard, yelled loudly in my mind, *"You're a procrastinator and a perfectionist!"*

I shrugged the voice off and muttered, "Someday I'll be perfect…"

The Procrastinator and the Perfectionist: Perfection Someday

It turns out my inner critic wasn't entirely wrong, and while the voice in my head could have been less mean, there was a good reason for all of this happening to me.

Research conducted showed that the brains of chronic procrastinators look and function differently from those of people who take action.

Using functional MRI technology, researchers were able to ascertain that procrastinators have a larger amygdala.

Now, the amygdala is part of the brain's limbic system and is in control of our primordial fight or flight response, which is an evolutionary function that is designed to keep us safe.

Why this is important to know is that when the amygdala is larger or more responsive, we're more likely to be hijacked by these evolutionary functions.

In other words, your brain perceives something to be dangerous or uncomfortable, and it hijacks your actions. Instead of doing the tasks at hand, your brain decides it doesn't want to have to deal with the tough feelings of frustration, failure, or even anger, and it decides you will just avoid the task entirely.

The same goes for your future!

Your brain decides that the future is uncertain and scary, and it makes the unilateral decision to avoid doing anything that will facilitate growth or forward momentum into the future (Weiler, 2018).

Of course, none of this is rational, but you need to remember that your amygdala deals with all things primordial, and that means you're better off trying to rationalize with a tantruming toddler than you are with your primordial brain.

This statement is not meant to discourage you or be used as an excuse for your procrastination because perfectionism is a choice, as are most of your actions and behaviors.

Let's go back to the tantruming toddler metaphor…

When a toddler experiences big emotions, they become frustrated and angry, and eventually, all these emotions turn into a meltdown that is fueled by fear.

These meltdowns can come in short bursts of outward behavioral displays or as hours-long episodes that can leave most parents utterly confused as to what to do to calm the storm.

Experienced childminders will tell you that distraction and redirection are key, and the same is true for your brain.

Taming Your Inner Toddler: Distract and Redirect, the 5-Second Rule

Mel Robbins is an American lawyer and motivational speaker who has experienced depression, anxiety, and perfectionism herself.

Through her own healing journey, she has developed techniques that work well, fast, and have lasting results.

But Robbins' techniques are not founded in mumbo-jumbo. She created exercises that apply neurological science and habit formation techniques to inspire and help thousands of people all over the world.

The 5-Second Rule is an incredibly useful tool to help overcome anxiety, take power back from your amygdala, and make spot decisions.

We all have moments in our lives when our inner toddler – our amygdala – takes over, repressing logical thought and forcing us into a state of survival.

The *5-Second Rule* works in three easy steps that are as brilliant as they are simple.

How It Works

Once you have identified that your amygdala is in control, you need to distract it so that your logical brain can take over and make a decision.

The issue with distraction is that perfectionism has taught you to be the master of distraction because you fear making a decision or the consequences of any decision you do make.

And this is where redirection and action take over.

Practicing the *5-Second Rule* will help you to reclaim control over your primordial brain, act, and then redirect, but it's going to take practice.

Robbins explains her technique in a way that is simple to understand (2017):

The *5-Second Rule* is simple. If you have the instinct to act on a goal, you must physically move within 5 seconds, or your brain will kill it. The moment you feel an instinct or a desire to act on a goal or a commitment, use the Rule.

When you feel yourself hesitating before doing something that you know you should do, count 5-4-3-2-1-GO and move towards action.

When we speak about a "goal" in this exercise, we are speaking about any action or decision that is causing you to procrastinate.

Come to think of it; we could use procrastinating about doing this exercise as an example.

You sit down wanting to do it, but your perfectionism takes over, and you realize that to do it really well, you need more time, and your thoughts begin to whirl… Instead of allowing your perfectionism to take over, count to five, and complete this exercise!

Method

So, you're ready to get started with the first exercise in this book?

Great!

Well done!

There is a very specific reason I have chosen this exercise as the first of many you will do, and that is because you will need to use it a lot throughout this book and your journey to transforming perfectionism into a superpower.

Every exercise in this book is a goal that should be achieved so that you can harness your own transformative abilities, and goals are our number one procrastination victims.

By practicing the *5-Second Rule*, you are essentially teaching your brain to act and then formulate rather than hesitate and procrastinate.

If you have been in a state of procrastination for a while, or if you are agonizing over even the smallest decisions, you may need to start by physically forcing yourself to move after your countdown.

To do this, you're going to need to take time every day, at least five times a day, to stop what you're doing, stand up, count backward from 5, and when you reach zero, jump!

Steps

1. Identify that you are procrastinating or that your amygdala has taken over.

2. Identify the thought. For example, "These dishes need to be done!"

3. Count backward slowly and methodically, starting at 5 – 5, breathe; 4, breathe; 3, breathe; 2, breathe; 1, breathe…

4. Now move toward your goal immediately. Don't hesitate; don't take another breath; just move. For example, "Pack your dishwasher and switch it on."

It is important that you move toward every goal and every procrastinated task this way, but only as they enter your mind so that you can train your brain to act on positive or constructive thoughts.

If we use my wall painting incident as an example, instead of standing and agonizing over how well it could be painted, what techniques were best, or what color best reflected my neighborhood, I should have acted.

And, I did!

Because the *5-Second Rule* works every time.

Flipping the Switch: How to Control Your Primordial Brain

Controlling your primordial brain can be a challenge.

You see, when you procrastinate on a task or replace it with something else, like binge-watching a series, you're creating a reward for your behavior.

Now, when we form habits, certain steps need to be taken for the habit to form.

Your brain cannot distinguish between a good habit and a bad habit; it simply gets fed the steps and forms the habit.

These steps, in order, are: a cue, action, routine, and reward.

The human brain requires all of these steps to create a habit – continue this behavior for a little under a month, and you will have a pretty solid habit in place.

Remove one of these steps, and a habit will never form.

Neat?

Right?

When you choose to avoid a task and replace doing the task with something else, you're inadvertently creating a habit.

Let's break this down, so it's easier to understand:

- I should do this task – take the cue.
- I am thinking about the task but doing nothing other than thinking – the action.

- I avoid the task by doing something that eases my anxiety – the routine.

- I have temporarily calmed my anxiety – the reward.

The issue with a habit is that we perpetuate our actions without much thought at all.

It's like brushing your teeth – you just brush them and are done.

The only time you actually think about brushing your teeth is when something changes in the chain of your habit.

This change could be a new toothbrush, a different flavor of toothpaste, new surroundings, and so on.

So how do we break the procrastination habit loop?

We think about it, and we replace the reward!

Method

Name the cue/behavior	
Name the reward	
Name the consequence	
Name a new behavior	
Name a new reward	

Here is an example of how you could fill this table.

Name the cue/behavior	*I avoid cutting the lawn.*
Name the reward	*I avoid dealing with my fear of bugs and pests.*
Name the consequence	*The lawn overgrows, and bugs and pests become worse.*
Name a new behavior	*The lawn will be cut every Sunday at 14:00. My alarm is set for this time, and I will use the 5-Second Rule.*
Name a new reward	*The lawn will be kept short and manicured, lowering the chances of bug and pest infestations.*

The Bigger Picture: Getting Things Done Using the Fearless-15

You now know that your procrastination tendencies have very little to do with laziness and a lot to do with different processes that are happening in your brain.

Being a perfectionist means getting stuck for various reasons, and these reasons can range from self-doubt to a crippling fear of failure.

The only way you are ever going to stop procrastinating your future is to help yourself become unstuck.

The exercises above are the first two steps in breaking the ties that bind you.

Having said that, acting without too much thought works only some of the time, and some tasks or goals you have been procrastinating on will require you to think about not only what you are procrastinating on but why you are procrastinating in the first place.

The Fearless-15 is designed to help you set aside time every single day to prioritize the important tasks you have been avoiding.

In addition, fifteen minutes is just enough time for you to work on a task until its conclusion without causing you too much anxiety.

Remember to set a reminder and an alarm and use your first exercise in this book, *The 5-Second Rule*, so that you act on your Fearless-15 immediately.

Method

1. Identify a critical task that you are avoiding. Use the exercise above, *Flipping the Switch*, to prioritize tasks in order of most important to least important.

   Here's the best part of this exercise… Unless a procrastinated task is going to land you in trouble with your job, finances, or relationship, you can choose the easiest one on the list first.

   If, however, one or more of these tasks are landing you in a lot of hot water, you're going to need to ascertain which of them is the most important and tackle this one first.

2. Schedule your Fearless-15. Make sure you are not sabotaging yourself by choosing a busy time of the day. Remember to listen to your intuition, and then commit to a time using the 5-Second Rule. Pop this time into your schedule every day of the week, adjusting your start time according to your individual scheduling needs.

3. Uncover your fears. Sometimes your procrastination can lead you into a huge amount of trouble, and because you fear the trouble you're in, you avoid having to deal with the task and the fear.

   The thing about fear is that it can only be overcome by facing it head-on and being honest about what has happened.

4. Establish your intentions. So, you have acknowledged you're procrastinating, uncovered why you are procrastinating, and have scheduled your Fearless-15; now is the time to set your reward or your intention.

   Having an intention or reward is important, not just for a habit loop to form, but so that you can understand the *why* behind what you're doing.

   These *whys* don't necessarily need to be profound; you'll find profundity while doing the tasks, but you do need an intention.

   An example of this might be, "I'm setting aside 15 minutes per day to clear out my bedroom of clutter and clean it. My intention is to create a sanctuary for myself so that I have a place to unwind at the end of the day. I have realized a cluttered environment is a big contributor to my stress and anxiety."

5. Pick a task and stick to it… Now act.

   The second your reminder goes off, count backward from 5; get up, and act. You may forget you ever needed to do your Fearless-15 in the beginning, and that is fine.

   If you have forgotten, stop what you're doing and reschedule for a later time during the day.

   You're only allowed to do this once, though, so be mindful and realistic about your rescheduled time.

   Remember, there is no guarantee of tomorrow, so act!

6. Only take on one task at a time and continue with this task every day until completion.

    If you are behind on opening your mail and paying your accounts, sit down for 15 minutes every Fearless-15 session and open one envelope, read the contents, act on the contents, and file or throw away the completed envelope, then grab another envelope.

    You're training your brain to be systematic with its processes and to face fear, anxiety, and overwhelm head-on so that you can utilize your stress for its intended purpose – to get things done!

Procrastination and perfectionism take time to overcome.

You've formed a habit, and that habit needs to be replaced by something better and more proactive for your progress and growth.

You're going to need to be disciplined and not rely on your motivation, because motivation is a temporary state of being.

The good news is that habits don't take forever to form, nor do they take forever to be replaced. Keep going with these exercises, and soon enough, you're going to find yourself becoming a master of procrastinating procrastination!

CHAPTER 2:

Harnessing Your Inner Achiever – Creating Your Flow State Finding Your Flow

Life presents us with a whole lot of obstacles to overcome so that we can learn and grow through experience.

The issue with the human race is that we tend to become hypercritical of ourselves.

Our once astronaut-dreaming, superhero-flying selves become self-aware and preoccupied with fitting in, being better than others, or simply keeping ourselves safe from all harm, including embarrassment.

I'd like you to take a moment to think back to when you were a young child, or, if you cannot remember, take the time to observe young kids.

Watch how they go about their tasks – coloring a picture, building sand castles, and interacting with their environment.

Notice how they seem to become completely absorbed by the task they are doing and how blissfully unaware they are of what the end product *should* look like.

Rather, their attention is focused on the process and how their movements are coordinating to create whatever it is that is in their minds.

This process is called a "flow state," and it is really important for harnessing your inner achiever and snapping out of a perfectionist state of mind.

Before I get into what a flow state is or how you can use it to your advantage, I would like you to take a moment to reflect upon the following statement, "Everything first starts with a thought…"

Whether you're aware of it or not, every movement, every breath – literally everything you do – begins with a thought.

Now I hear you saying, "I don't think about breathing!"

Technically you do; you're just not aware of the thought in the same way you are not aware of your thoughts for any other automated task.

If you have ever experienced crippling anxiety or a panic attack, you will be acutely aware of how you actually have control over your breathing and how you can harness your breath to your advantage – but more on that later.

For now, I would like you to become aware that your thoughts dictate everything in your life, and since you can gain control over your thoughts, you are capable of just about anything if you have the right mindset.

It Starts With a Thought

Perfectionism aside, we all have days where we feel focused and sharp, and other days where we feel like we're wading through a bleak fog that obscures our every thought and action.

When we are focused and sharp, our actions and intentions are clear, facilitating a natural state of creation, and this is what a flow state is – the easy exchange of thought into action.

When we are in a state of flow, our movements seem to become fluid, and our mind is crystal clear… There's no inner critic in sight!

During a flow state, our brains experience a number of changes, including producing dopamine, our brain's built-in reward system.

When dopamine neurotransmitters kick in, we naturally feel pleasure or motivation, and as such, we're more compelled to complete a task.

Research shows that when in a flow state, the brain's locus coeruleus-norepinephrine (lc-ne) system is activated (Linden et al., 2020).

Now, I am not going to bore you with long scientific explanations, but the lc-ne system is responsible for a whole lot of neurobiological processes, including our ability to self-regulate stress.

With the lc-ne system in charge during a flow state, the brain goes into a regulation mode, facilitating engagement and decision-making, which is why you are able to complete a task without emotions taking over (Linden et al., 2020).

In other words, the different areas of your brain are able to communicate better with each other, and while they're communicating, your inner critic is drowned out.

When combined with proper goal setting and action, a flow state helps you to push your perfectionist aside, silence your inner critic, and unlock your inner achiever.

The reason for this goes beyond your brain's natural dopamine reward system, though.

When you can work in and master a state of flow, you're more likely to develop a sense of self-fulfillment and intrinsic motivation that rids you of a perpetual state of *should* and swaps it for a deeper sense of *want* and improves your performance and efficiency.

Ridding Yourself of Should: An Exercise in Priority and Delegation

Everyone gets stuck on the things they should do from time to time.

It's inevitable, really, especially with the frenetic pace of modern life!

The issue with *shoulds* is that we can end up feeling stuck because of all of the endless tasks we burden ourselves with versus being realistic about the things we need to do to be happy.

I mean, you should be eating a healthy meal every day. But if your schedule is really full, you hate cooking, and the cost of having a month's worth of healthy meals delivered to your door is the same as shopping for your ingredients, then you could delegate.

The issue with perfectionism is that we feel we should do things or believe no one can do these things better than we can. And the irony is that we avoid having to do the tasks in the first place because our schedule is so full of *shoulds*.

Don't believe me… "I should be eating a healthy meal every day, but my schedule is full, and I'm sure I could cook this healthy meal option myself, but it is 9:00 p.m., I am hungry, and I should eat something, so I will order fast food. I will go to the shops tomorrow to buy healthy food to cook."

And when tomorrow, 9:00 p.m., arrives, we rinse and repeat the cycle because we *should* have gone to the store, but we didn't because our schedule is full, and we could cook this healthy meal ourselves…

Do you see how it should work?

They get you stuck, and once you're stuck, it takes a whole lot of energy to get yourself unstuck.

So, how do you deal with all of your *shoulds*?

Method

You schedule a Fearless-15 so that you can complete the exercise below!

What do I believe I *should* be doing?	Could this task be delegated?	What is my intention for this task?	Delegate by?

We can use healthy meals as an example.

"I should be eating a healthy meal every day. I could delegate this task by ordering one month's worth of healthy meals to my door. My intention for this task is to ensure I am nourishing my body properly. This task will be delegated in my next Fearless-15."

Achieving a Flow State: Riding the Wave to Success

Your urge to avoid tasks is deeply rooted in fear of not being able to complete a task perfectly or that you will appear to be a failure if you don't perfectly do what needs to be done.

Fear is an emotion, and like all other emotions, it only lasts 90 seconds before fading. Everything beyond your initial emotion is a conscious choice, even if you don't feel like it is, and a lot of what we feel is programmed by habit.

If I were to call your name and, as you turned around, toss a glass of water at you, the very next time I called your name, you would either not turn around, or you would flinch, regardless of whether or not I had a glass in my hand.

Your brain programs itself to act or react in a certain way when dealing with emotions, and you're going to need to change your actions so that you can achieve a flow state.

An easy way to deprogram your learned responses is to ride the wave that is your emotion, practicing mindfulness and acceptance as the emotion passes.

Urge surfing is a dialectical behavioral therapy (DBT) tool that allows you to acknowledge, manage, flow through, and then act on your intentions.

This technique will take some practice to master, but once you're an emotion surfing pro, it will become easy to avoid your avoidant behaviors.

Method

The human brain is only capable of experiencing six basic emotions.

Now, you can experience more than one emotion at a time, and when these emotions combine, a new emotion is created. The number of combined emotions, however, is finite and, as such, limited to 25.

These six basic emotions are: happiness, sadness, disgust, fear, surprise, and anger (Cherry, 2021).

With these emotions in mind, use the steps below to help achieve a state of flow whenever you feel like your procrastination or perfectionism may take over:

1. The first step in riding your emotion wave is to acknowledge the basic emotion. For the perfectionist, the most common emotion experienced is a combination of fear and surprise, which results in anxiety or nervousness.

2. Once you have identified your emotion, you will name it. If your thoughts are whirling or you're gripped by anxiety, say your emotion out loud. "I am anxious!"

3. Take a deep breath once you have identified and acknowledged your emotion. Don't allow your thoughts to cast judgment or even comment on your emotion. Simply accept that you are in a temporary state. If your thoughts are persistently critical, keep repeating, "Emotions are a temporary state."

4. Continue to focus on your breath, breathing through the physical feelings you are experiencing. Inhale through your nose and exhale through your mouth in evenly timed, smooth breaths.

5. Notice as your emotion reaches its peak and acknowledge it once more, but this time, make sure to use the past tense of your emotion – "I was anxious."

6. Return your focus to your breath and remind yourself that emotions are a temporary state.

7. During the fall of your emotion wave, alter your breathing pattern. Inhale deeply through your nose, hold your breath for two seconds, and exhale through your mouth. Allow your emotion to pass like a wave breaching the shores.

8. Now start counting: 5, breathe, 4, breathe, 3, breathe, 2, breathe, 1, breathe and take action by starting your task.

Mindfulness: Train Your Brain to Flow

Training your brain to flow is tough when you are a perfectionist and have a tendency to get caught up in the details.

Perfectionism can drive you to get caught in a loop that analyzes the steps it will take to complete a project rather than focusing on the movements or actions required to get things done.

When you enjoy doing something, a flow state happens naturally, but perfectionism can often rob you of even those tasks that make you happy.

You will need to retrain your brain to flow so that you can find joy in the tasks you are doing – yes… Even the mundane ones!

The problem is that when we are younger, not only do we get caught up in how well a task *should* be done, but we also get caught up in labeling certain tasks as pleasant or unpleasant.

We're told that certain things are chores, and the very word "chore" means something that is tedious but necessary.

The reality is that any task or action you do during the day can be done in a flow state, and the brain is most comfortable, most efficient, and happiest when you allow it to flow.

This exercise is to be completed with three results in mind: To practice and allow your brain to enter a flow state, to commit to the steps required for a task, and to see the bigger picture as the end result.

Taken from art therapy practices, training your brain to flow is enjoyable, messy, and allows your curious inner child to come out and play while providing you with valuable adult life skills.

Items Required

- Several magazines, mailbox flyers, newspapers, or scrap pieces of paper from unsoiled food packaging. If you would like to get creative, you could even cut up old clothes, towels, tin foil, and so on. The world is your oyster when it comes to the materials you can use.

- A line drawing of a picture – enter the words "line drawing" into your preferred online search engine. Open the images tab, close your eyes, and scroll for the count of five. Now open your eyes and pick the third image from the top.

- Print the line drawing picture – an A4-sized printout will work, to begin with. You can graduate to larger sizes once you have the hang of this exercise.

- A stick of glue.

- Scissors if you are using fabric or food packaging.

- Any container large enough to house a couple of pieces of scrap paper.

Method

You will need some basic household objects for this exercise.

These objects require little to no thought, and the size of your brain-training exercise doesn't matter.

Remember, your aim is not perfection; it is getting the task done.

1. Gather all of your supplies and place them on a non-cluttered working surface. A kitchen counter, dining table, or even living room or bedside table will do.

2. Set a timer for 15 minutes.

3. Place your container in the center of the table.

4. Grab one of your scrap items. Don't think about it; just pick up a random item.

5. Begin to tear or cut your scrap item into smaller pieces, placing each of these smaller pieces into the container. Again, no thought is required… Tear and pop it into the container.

6. Grab another scrap item and repeat Step 5 until your container is about half full.

7. Place your hand into the container and jumble up the contents. Take a moment to be mindful, feeling the different textures and seeing the different colors settle into a different space in the container.

8. Put your container and any unused scrap items to one side but within arm's reach.

9. Place your printed line drawing in front of you and open your glue stick.

10. Now, without looking, put your hand into the container and take a piece of your torn and cut-up scraps. Don't worry if you grab more than one; you can place the other pieces to one side and forgo a hand-dip next round.

11. Get your stick of glue, cover the back of your scrap piece, and place it randomly on your line drawing.

12. Place your hand back into the container or pick up one of your excess pieces of scrap from your previous picking round and repeat Step 11.

13. Continue to repeat Steps 10 and 11 until your entire line drawing is covered in scrap materials. If you find yourself thinking about where to stick your pieces, close your eyes, take a deep breath, and stick the scrap down with your eyes closed.

14. Allow your line drawing sufficient time to dry, about 30 minutes.

15. Finally, hold your collaged picture up and examine it. Do you see how all of the pieces of meaningless trash have created something beautiful? Do you acknowledge that this is a physical representation of how methodically performing one micro-action after the next still leads to creation?

Your inner achiever requires you to take back control of the intricate communication balances that occur in your brain.

You need to learn to flow through all of your activities and banish the very notion that anything in life is a "chore."

Everything you do in your life is a set of methodical micro-actions that create a result.

Even procrastination and perfectionism fall into this micro-action category, but the result is anxiety – a whole lot of anxiety, stress, and incompleteness – rather than a proactive outcome that helps you to learn and grow.

CHAPTER 3:

The Creation of a Meaningful Inner Voice

Our inner voice goes by different names: self-talk, verbal thinking, inner speech, internal monologue, and sometimes a whole lot of words that cannot be used in a published book.

This inner voice develops over our childhood and is a collection of cognition, behavior, self-regulation, how we were raised, the adults in our lives, and other developmental and psychological factors (Alderson-Day & Fernyhough, 2015).

Some people don't have an inner voice or aren't cognitively aware of their internal dialogue, but I'm sure you know that those who develop perfectionist tendencies experience inner speech loud and clear!

In addition, inner voices can be experienced in different ways: as your own voice, someone else's voice, numerous voices, numbers, pictures, and so on.

Inner dialogues are still a hot topic of discussion among psychologists and cognitive neuroscientists today, and while a lot of research is still being done, one thing that is definite is that our inner voice plays a big role in human cognition (Schroeder et al., 2021).

Human cognition is the mental process that occurs as we experience the world around us and is a collection of our senses, perceptions, experiences, and thoughts.

The great thing about cognition is that when you change one component of this collection, your cognition changes. For example, if you change your perception, you will experience your environment in a completely different way.

A great way to think about cognition is to walk into a room that is familiar to you. Instead of navigating this room as you normally would, blindfold yourself and try to move around your environment.

Your entire experience of a familiar room will be different once you have removed or changed one component – removing one of your senses.

For Yourself or Against Yourself?

Now that you have a better idea of what your inner voice is, let's dive into that nagging inner critic that tends to push us into perfectionism.

Your inner critic is nothing more than a reflection of the thoughts that make up your internal dialogue.

An inner voice can be for you or against you, and if you choose for it to be against you, it will be the cause of maladaptive behaviors, cognitive bias, and self-limiting beliefs.

You will notice I used the word "choose" in the sentence above, and that is because you *do* have a choice in how you deal with your inner critic, short-circuiting the thoughts that drive your perfectionist behaviors.

Think of your inner critic as a school bully that hounds you with a constant stream of words to discourage you from acting in your own best interest.

With enough time and attentive listening to this inner critic, your own thoughts can damage your confidence, self-esteem, success, relationships, and performance... Hello, procrastination!

When you choose to listen to your inner critic, you are essentially creating a relationship with yourself that is distrustful.

Think about it – you wouldn't trust anyone who spoke to you in the same way you speak to yourself!

There is a common myth that if you do not listen to your inner critic, you will lose touch with yourself or start to engage in risk-taking behavior. Rest assured that your inner critic has nothing to do with your ability to define right from wrong, nor does it have anything to do with who you are.

Your inner critic is a collection of thoughts you have formulated throughout your childhood… nothing more… nothing less.

And, everyone has nagging negative thoughts and even doubts from time to time; the difference between being for yourself or against yourself is what you do with these thoughts.

I remember being at a local park once. Kids were playing on the perfectly manicured grass, and while I was supposed to have my nose in my book, I couldn't help but be present at the moment, observing the world around me.

Among all the happy giggles and shrills of excitement, one voice cried out, "I'm so stupid!"

I watched as a young child's minder walked up to them, getting down to the child's level.

"What is the problem?" she asked, wiping away tears.

The child, frustrated and defeated, dissolved into a flurry of tears and words about how ugly, stupid, and uncoordinated they were.

Without skipping a beat, the childminder said, "Let's take a deep breath!"

The child breathed deeply, mimicking their minder.

"Right," the childminder said, "let me ask you a question. Would you say any of the words you just used to describe your best friend?"

"No…" the child began to wail again.

"What would you tell them if they were struggling like you?"

The child answered with enthusiasm, "I would tell them how smart and cool they are!"

"Then that's what you should tell yourself! You're the smartest, coolest kid I know because you are your own best friend."

These words stuck with me, especially since I was actively recovering from banishing my own inner critic, and I carry this mantra around with me to this day.

I believe everyone would be able to silence their inner critic if they just realized that they were their own best friend and repeated it over and over again…

"You're the smartest, coolest kid I know!"

The Thought Challenge Checklist: Negative Thoughts Be Gone!

Your inner dialogue and the thoughts that accompany it in your mind can have a profound impact on how you feel and behave.

Many of these thoughts are rooted in our self-belief system and create Automatic Negative Thoughts (ANTs).

These thoughts are sometimes really difficult to control because they are habitual by nature, and we only become aware of them when our self-esteem takes a knock, or we begin to analyze our behaviors.

When we become aware of our ANTs, we can begin to challenge them, setting our course to one that embraces learning and encourages and uplifts us.

The exercise below is designed to help you identify your ANTs and will give you the tools to replace negativity with positive statements.

Method

I have placed an example in the table below for you so that you have a better idea of how to challenge your thoughts.

This table can be used whenever you identify a negative thought or as part of your daily journaling practices.

Challenging ANTs is a difficult task because they are connected to our self-belief system, and you may find yourself avoiding this task. If you find yourself procrastinating in this exercise, use the *5-Second Rule* to get it done.

Trigger: What happened before the thought?	ANT: What was the thought, and what dialogue occurred?	New thought: What would I tell my best friend or a child?
I didn't journal today.	I can't commit to anything. I am so weak and ill-disciplined.	I have the tools to complete this task. I am sitting down for a Fearless-15 right now!

Make sure to adapt your language so that it works for you. For example, some people who are experiencing negative thoughts will use the "you" language, "You are such a failure," while others will use the "I" language, "I am such a failure," and others will use their name.

Adapting the language you use when banishing and replacing negative thoughts is a powerful way to speak directly with your mind, letting it know that you are entering into a dialogue with your thoughts specifically.

Parent, Adult, and Child Model: Transactional Analysis for Communication

Transactional analysis is a method that uncovers how people communicate with themselves, others, and their environment.

It is based on the theory that human beings communicate from three ego states – parent, adult, and child.

Each of these states can be further broken down into functional and non-functional states. For example, a parent state can be critical or nurturing, and a child state can be rebellious, free, or compliant.

When we are self-critical, we are using language that is non-functional and forces our minds into a fearful, angry, or anxious state, hindering our ability to focus on what needs to be done.

Method

The worksheet below is designed to help you uncover what ego state you are using to communicate from and gives you the opportunity to take a breath and select the type of ego state you would like to communicate from.

It's important that you acknowledge that internal dialogues, while they feel one-sided, are actually two-sided, as your inner voice is communicating with and driving an external force – your behavior.

All inner dialogues should be viewed as two-way dialogues that open communication channels.

Worksheet Key

The key below gives you a brief insight into the types of ego states and whether they are functional or non-functional.

You will need to replace each non-functional state with a functional one.

When in doubt over whether or not your inner voice is critical or not, revert back to the example in this chapter and ask yourself, *Does this statement sound like the coolest kid I know?*

Critical parent, non-functional: aggressive, controlling, critical, degrading – "You're so stupid, you can't do this task!"

Nurturing parent, functional: caring, concerned, loving, understanding – "This task is tough, but I know you can do it if you try."

Adult functional: logical, non-judgmental, organized, factual – "I am busy with this task now; it will be completed within the hour."

Rebellious child, non-functional: boredom, distraction, procrastination, disobedience – "I hate this task; I don't feel like doing it; I will do something I like!"

Compliant child, non-functional: withdrawal, people pleaser, sulking, blaming, feeling hurt – "I have to do this task because no one else will do it properly. I will let everyone know I did the task the way it should be done!"

Free child, functional: curious, excited, free-spirited, expressive, enthusiastic – "This task looks tough, but I am going to make it fun and get it done!"

Thought	Current State	Desired State
I hate having to compile a grocery list. I feel so stupid when I forget an item!	Rebellious child	Nurturing parent: *It can be so frustrating when we forget an item, but a quick trip to the store can fix that!*

Kindergartener: I'm Not Listening... La-la-la-la-la!

The issue with listening to your inner critic is that it robs you of your joy in just about anything you do in your life.

That critical inner voice wasn't always there, though, and when you were younger, you probably had the confidence of a peacock on a warm spring day.

Most children, when they are young, unencumbered, and have not yet been introduced to the world of shame or guilt, believe they can do just about anything.

Sure, they may have moments of self-doubt, but some encouragement from an adult in their lives or a friend doing the task first is usually enough of a confidence boost to take the leap and try things out.

Your inner critic likes to mock, tease, and, to be blunt, bully you, and if you think back to your younger days, an adult probably gave you two pieces of advice: Ignore the bully or counter them with a swift, "So what!"

Now, I know this all sounds easier said than done, especially when that nagging voice gets involved at every single step of your project.

In the exercise above, you learned that communication always occurs from one of your ego states, and your inner critic loves to break your ego.

The thing with your inner critic is that sometimes it will build you up first, only to use your best efforts to destroy you later on.

So, how do you go about putting your inner critic back in their place and silencing them once and for all?

The first thing you will need to do is identify this voice in the first place.

What does your inner critic say?

What is its favorite bullying tactic?

Can you physically feel your energy depleting as your inner critic takes over?

Do you feel bored, stuck, or even fatigued?

In the early phases of silencing your inner critic, they will probably escalate, getting louder in your mind and pressuring you to crack under the harshness of their words.

The best way to deal with your inner critic, especially in these escalating phases, is to tap into your inner child, using the confidence you had all those years ago.

Method

Before you respond to your inner critic, you're going to need to identify why they are talking to you in the first place.

This first step requires a little bit of self-awareness and mindfulness so that you can counter what they have to say.

Use this exercise when your inner critic's words don't require deeper insight. When these words do need deeper insight, write them down and schedule a Fearless-15 session so that you can uncover what limiting beliefs are fueling the words.

Every other time, it's important that you dismiss your inner critic quickly by using your inner kindergartener.

Use the phrases below or make up your own custom phrases to get your inner critic to shut up quickly!

Phrase	Reason
Big deal!	Seriously, who really cares about the mean voice in your head?
And what are you?!	Separating your inner critic from yourself helps quiet it pretty quickly.
So what?	Your inner critic disappears pretty quickly when you don't allow them to go into the finer details.
Who cares?	You don't want to care about what your inner critic is saying, so don't. Rather, ask, "Who cares?"
It doesn't matter!	Unless your profession actually demands perfection from you because lives are at risk, mistakes don't matter.
Why not?	This is especially useful when your inner critic says you can't do things. And, when they reply with all of the reasons you can't do something, reply with, "So what?" or "Who cares?"

Use the blank spaces on this table to fill in your own rebuttals and ways to silence your inner critic.

Silencing your inner critic, finding healthy ways of communicating with yourself, and challenging automatic negative thoughts are critical for you to not only overcome perfectionism but to regain control of your mental well-being.

Once you begin to silence all of the things that you say to yourself and take steps to build a healthy relationship where you value yourself as your own best friend, it becomes easier to build self-confidence.

Once you are confident and sure of your abilities, all other aspects of your life become easier, more fulfilling, and can be approached with curiosity and excitement rather than anxiety and dread.

CHAPTER 4:

Snapping Out of Analysis Paralysis

Analysis paralysis… The process of thinking, overthinking, ruminating, and having the same thoughts and scenarios play over and over in your head.

Ruminating on thoughts is counterintuitive and provides you with absolutely no insight into the decisions you need to make.

It's like watching the same short film on repeat, hoping to uncover something you may have missed the first 50 times you watched it.

Getting stuck in the analysis is exhausting and overwhelming, and when your brain becomes fatigued, it shuts down, triggering a state of "paralysis."

We all know that the goal is to put some distance between us and the decision or to just make a decision and stick to it, but the decision-making process itself takes so much mental energy that we choose to avoid it entirely.

Here's the thing about the decisions we need to make throughout our lives: There are always going to be a number of options that are good or bad, and there's always the possibility of success or failure.

Life is full of unknown variables, and that means most of the decisions we have to make force us to step into the unknown.

An unknown is a scary place for most of us.

Our brain is wired to keep us safe, but for most people, the ability to trust our instincts has been overtaken by the need to outperform our peers.

Important, life-changing decisions require some time and consideration, but when we become stuck in ruminating thoughts and *what-ifs*, we end up making no decisions at all.

Analysis paralysis can look different for different people, with some people taking an exorbitant amount of time to research their best options and others handling the decision-making process and responding to someone else.

I once met a couple in the midst of a crisis because of a pair of shoes!

"Two weeks!" the wife proclaimed, exhausted. "Two entire weeks to pick a pair of shoes, and they all look and feel the same and have the same function!"

When I met up with her a couple of weeks later, I asked the wife what had happened with the shoe purchase. She told me that after walking around a mall and revisiting the same shops over and over again, she yelled a famous quote before storming out of the store to find a place where she could have a cup of coffee. Her husband joined her not long after, a new pair of shoes in hand.

I asked her what quote she used to snap her partner out of analysis paralysis…

"Life is short; eat the cake; buy the shoes!"

Buy the Shoes!

Giving into analysis paralysis is a bad idea, but then you probably already know that. Getting stuck in the perpetual large "what-ifs" gives way to analyzing even the smallest decisions until, eventually, you're stuck for hours on end trying to decide what pair of socks are best.

And, I'm not telling you this to make the situation worse, but even small decisions could end up being the wrong choice.

Why you get stuck in this endless loop of scenarios is pretty interesting, if not overwhelming, and it may not seem like it now, but it's actually easy to get out of.

Our brains are divided into two hemispheres that are connected by a whole lot of nerve fibers so that one side of the brain can communicate with the other.

The left side of our brain is responsible for analytical thought, including formulating words, sequencing, linear thinking, logic, and so on. The right side of our brain is the creative side and relies on intuition. Our right brain controls imagination, intuition, art, rhythm, and visualization, among other creative things.

When we have the decision to make, our left brain uses logic and thinking to come up with possible scenarios using reasoning. It then sends this message to the right brain so that an intuitive feeling can be ascertained.

The right brain then visualizes and imagines the situation, sending it back to the left brain for further analysis.

Now, the problem begins with intuitive thought processes and our inability to trust our intuition.

Instead of this process happening a couple of times before action, we work against our intuition, forcing our brains to reanalyze the situation over and over again until both the left and right sides of the brain hand the problem over to the amygdala, and… Hijack!

Our brains, tired of being forced to repeat their process over a decision, go into freeze mode, and we become paralyzed, unable to make a decision at all (Pignatiello et al., 2018).

In other words, we are willfully and purposefully interrupting our natural flow state and causing ourselves anxiety.

The problem with overthinking as a whole is that it is entirely unproductive and causes us so much more anxiety than it should.

Yes, life is about a series of decisions we need to make, but ultimately, we only have one choice – if we act, it's a choice, and if we don't, it's still a choice.

People who are motivated by a need to overachieve or perfectionists fall into this trap purely because of a fear of failing, and when fear takes over, it can be very difficult to make a choice.

The Problem: Using the Four P's to Uncover the Problem

Analysis paralysis doesn't just come into being one day.

It takes time and a lot of negative thinking for you to get into the habit of doubting yourself. While it feels like second nature now, you actually put a whole lot of hard work into the habit you're perpetuating.

Analysis paralysis almost always stems from our self-limiting beliefs, and CBT has uncovered methods to help you uncover not only where these beliefs began but also how to replace them with positive, action-oriented beliefs (Racine et al., 2015).

The Four Ps of this exercise are:

- Predisposing – whether or not there are any genetic or hereditary factors. For example, is anyone in your family predisposed to anxiety, depression, and so on?

- Precipitating – your experiences that trigger your behaviors. Were you bullied at school? Did you feel you needed to be perfect to be loved, and so on?

- Perpetuating – did anyone facilitate this behavior? For example, did you have a parent who encouraged you to be cautious? A helicopter parent, or maybe attending a school that demanded compliance?

- Protective – which of the above factors could contribute to you avoiding tasks as an emotional defense mechanism?

Method

Using the table below, analyze your behaviors so that you can uncover the reasons you are entering into analysis paralysis.

When completing this exercise, make sure to be mindful and conscious of what your self-limiting beliefs are so that you can use the exercise below to restructure these beliefs.

Complete the sentence above the table before completing each of the columns.

Make sure to dig into your automatic thoughts as a way to uncover what protective mechanisms you are using to avoid tasks presently.

This exercise can be used every time you find yourself entering into analysis paralysis.

I have completed the first table for you as an example of how you can use *The Four Ps* as an effective way to uncover your self-limiting beliefs.

The problem is… *I have a presentation due on the reduction of office waste as a way to decrease our environmental footprint. I haven't begun the presentation because I don't know what products are necessary for the smooth running of our office. Besides, I wasn't any good at this type of thing at school!*

Predisposing	Precipitating	Perpetuating	Protective	Self-Limiting Belief
None	It was expected of me to achieve 80% in all subjects as an acceptable pass rate.	My educators agreed that I was capable of achieving this mark, and it wasn't unreasonable.	I feel like my lack of knowledge in this area means I cannot produce a great presentation.	To be accepted, I need to perform to unreasonably high standards.

The problem is…

Predisposing	Precipitating	Perpetuating	Protective	Self-Limiting Belief

The problem is…

Predisposing	Precipitating	Perpetuating	Protective	Self-Limiting Belief

Lights... Camera... Action: Cognitive Restructuring

Socratic questioning is a technique that encourages you to not only challenge your thoughts – yes, those what-ifs as well – but also inspire action so that you can break out of your analysis loop.

As you now know, your thoughts are always present and fleeting, but for some reason, negative thoughts tend to want to hang around forever.

This is not a bad thing either because when you have lingering or repetitive negative thoughts, you also have the chance to challenge them!

This exercise has been designed to let you capture your thoughts, putting them down on paper so that you can ascertain whether or not they are accurate so that you can move past perpetual scenarios and onto the task at hand.

Method

While I have provided you with a worksheet below, this exercise can be done with any piece of paper and a pen or pencil to jot down your thoughts.

In fact, I encourage you to write down any thought that hinders your progress, not only because it can help you uncover why you are in analysis paralysis but also because it serves as a distraction.

Answer the questions below each time you experience analysis paralysis or a negative thought:

1. What is the thought?
2. Is this thought factual?
3. What are the facts?
4. What are not facts?
5. Is this thought an opinion?
6. What is my opinion?
7. What is the truth or fact about this thought?

This or That: Living With Decisions

Life is full of decisions you will need to make, and most of these decisions, simply put, cannot be made *for* you.

Of course, you can trust others to make some decisions, but how are you ever going to be truly happy if your life is based on the choices others make for you?

This is your life to live, and true contentment and inner peace come from doing the things we need to do and want to do to make ourselves happy.

The issue with analysis paralysis is that you become so caught up in the finer details of the decisions you need to make – yes, even the smallest ones – that you either become dependent on others to make these decisions for you or you avoid making a decision at all.

Learning to make a decision and committing to it is vitally important for your mental well-being, and learning to live with the smaller decisions you need to make will prepare you for making larger ones.

Here's the thing about life… A whole lot of what happens to us is completely out of our control.

In fact, the only control you do have is how you react to the things that happen, and that means you really only have one choice to make – to look for the positive in a decision or to be miserable in a decision.

You could go to your favorite restaurant to eat and still be thoroughly miserable with your decision while you wonder what the food would've been like at another restaurant. Or, you could choose to be present at the moment, enjoying the experience that has come with your choice.

Method

This or That is designed to help you practice acceptance and mindfulness and develop the ability to be present and content with your decisions.

It's important to note that this exercise is a form of radical acceptance, and as such, you may feel like procrastinating or canceling it all together.

You're going to need to draw on your self-discipline, using any or all of the exercises in the previous chapters to push yourself to get this task done.

To begin with, it's a good idea to select places and activities you are familiar with so that you can ease into the exercise.

Once you have practiced every step of the exercise and are confident you are ready, you can choose places and activities that are unfamiliar to you.

Finally, you can ask someone you trust to list activities and places they believe you would enjoy but that you are uncomfortable with. This will help you begin teaching yourself to move outside of your comfort zone.

1. You will need one container for each of the categories listed below.

2. You will also need to either print the table below or have some scrap paper and a pair of scissors on hand to cut out each item.

3. Select three places or activities from the categories below. Remember to make a choice based on comfort or familiarity first. You can graduate to the unfamiliar later.

4. Write down these activities, cutting each one out and placing it into the relevant containers. You may want to label your containers if you would like to dedicate an entire day to this exercise. For example, one container labeled activity, one container labeled food, and one labeled things to get done.

5. Set aside some time once a week to select one activity from your containers. Alternatively, choose to dedicate an entire day to your decisions and pick enough activities to fill your day.

I have added examples to the first line of your table so that you have a better understanding of the exercise.

Activity	Food	Get Done
Go to the grocery store with a list.	Cook spaghetti bolognaise.	Deeply clean the oven.

When selecting a category and completing the exercise, make sure you are mindful of your experience.

Look for the positives, incorporate all of your senses, and make a conscious decision to silence your inner critic.

Always remember, these exercises are not meant to be done perfectly; they're meant to get done and enjoyed without judgment or expectation.

Experiencing analysis paralysis is frustrating and is a combination of trained neurobiological processes, self-limiting beliefs, and a fear that any decision made will be wrong.

Breaking the loop of communication between your left and right brain, and ensuring you commit to being mindful while participating in all of the experiences life has to offer will improve your well-being, and assist you in developing a mindset for success.

CHAPTER 5:

Embracing Failure for Growth

An all-or-nothing mindset does very little for personal growth but does wonders for helping develop our self-limiting beliefs, driving our procrastination tendencies, and basically handing our inner-critic a big 'ole megaphone.

The constant pressure to succeed or to get things done perfectly often forces us to put our blinders on and overlook the bigger issues we are facing. Because, let's face it, it's far easier to avoid the elephant in the room, no matter how much space it's taking up.

In fact, perfectionism often completely masks the glaringly obvious problems we are creating for ourselves – so much so that we turn our own lives upside down in pursuit of a complete human myth.

It's the whole toppling dominoes analogy, isn't it?

You can choose to remove one domino from the stack so that the line stops cascading, or you can leave every domino in place until a complete picture falls.

So, what is it that we are trying to avoid by pulling the domino from its stack?

Failure!

Or, at the very least, learning to embrace failure.

The tech giant IBM has a philosophy when it comes to innovating product and service offerings: "Fail fast so that you can learn fast." And, there is a method in this madness because each time we fail at a task, we are provided with a multitude of insights, most of which are incredibly helpful in improving our processes, efficiency, and flow.

Certainly, when we were much younger, we adopted a "fail fast" attitude without much conscious thought at all. We just go about repeating the same tasks over and over again until we get things done.

Embrace Failure Fast and Learn Fast

Somewhere in our childhood, our tenacity, and our penchant for making mistakes lose their appeal with the adults in our lives, and cooing words of, "Oh, try again, honey," are replaced with impatient foot taps and, "Just let me do it because you're taking forever!"

We enter school and are graded on our educational, sporting, and performance efforts, often with enormous fear that we will get things wrong and be handed a failing grade.

We're conditioned to believe that failure is negative, and we're often punished for making mistakes, all of which leads to us hiding our mistakes by blaming our circumstances, other people, or even ourselves.

We are taught that failure is the big bad in the room, and we are to avoid it at all costs, lest we be called bad ourselves!

The fact of the matter is that failure is imperative to human development, and without it, the truly bad stuff happens.

Don't you believe me?

Studies show that failure is necessary for growth and that it is our persistence through failure that allows us to learn important fine and gross motor skills in the developmental periods of our lives (Loscalzo, 2014).

The truly astounding thing is that most of us are led to believe we are done developing when we move out of adolescence as if some switch is flipped in our brains that says, "That's it; no more learning or growth for you!"

This thought process was the standard for many years until modern science revealed we have the capacity and, indeed, the need to continue to grow and develop throughout our lives.

That means every stage of your life: pregnancy, infancy, toddler years, childhood, puberty, older adolescence, adulthood, middle age, and the senior years – requires trial and error to develop and grow.

Even babies in utero practice and fail to breathe until the day they leave their protected space!

And here's the thing about failure… Whether you fear it or not, one thing is absolutely certain – failure is as inevitable as your blinking, breathing, and heart beating. So why not embrace it?

Why not step away from the ideology that failure is the worst thing that could happen to you and learn to fail fast, try fast, and grow fast?

Make a Mess: Failure for the Bigger Picture

Perfectionism can have us spending a lot of time forgetting about the bigger picture and getting caught up in the details.

We forget that perfection lies in imperfection and that anything we deem to be beautiful, satisfying, or even, dare I say it, perfect!

Our fear of failure can begin in childhood or be a result of being stuck in survival mode.

Whatever the reason for your fear, it's important that you let go of your failure so that you can embrace how beautifully messy life actually is.

In other words, you will need to come to peace with the fact that the bigger picture doesn't always require precision or perfection – it simply requires you to commit to a decision and perform an action.

Failure for the Bigger Picture is an exercise that requires some preparation but is a whole lot of fun and will allow you to tap into your inner child.

In addition, this exercise will help you see that perfection is not needed for something to be completed, nor is it required to create something beautiful.

Based on art therapy practices, this exercise taps into your flow state while incorporating your senses and encouraging mindfulness.

Items Required

- A large piece of scrap paper.

- An outdoor area.

- Paints in different colors.

- Paintbrush or brushes.

- Jars of water.

- A rag to wipe off your brushes.

- Old clothes that you don't mind getting dirty.

Method

1. Go into an outdoor area and lay out your sheet of paper.

2. Fill your jars with water and get your paintbrush and rags.

3. Open each of your paint jars and arrange them close together.

4. Dip your brush in one of your paints. Make sure your brush is properly saturated.

5. Take a deep breath.

6. Notice the color of your paintbrush. Does the color resonate with you? What does the paint smell like? Does the color bring back memories?

7. Now, close your eyes, take another deep breath, and flick your brush so that the paint splatters on your sheet of paper.

8. Open your eyes and take a look at the splatter. Do you see any shapes or patterns in the paint?

9. Don't take too much time to analyze your paint splatter, and don't allow your thoughts to take over. Simply look at the paint with curiosity, and then move on to the next step.

10. Wash your paintbrush off.

11. Dip your paintbrush into a different color.

12. Now, repeat steps 6 through 9.

13. Alternate your colors with each paint flick, and use each color a minimum of five times.

14. Once you have completed this exercise, allow your paper to dry properly.

15. Next, take your paper indoors and place it on a flat surface, hang it on the wall, or place it on the floor and stand on a chair so that you can look down at it.

16. Do you see how the paint splatter has formed beautiful art?

ACT, Failure, and Fear Crusher: Smashing Your Fears

Acceptance and commitment therapy (ACT) is designed to help you overcome your fears.

It uses a combination of action, acceptance, and mindfulness to help you overcome your anxieties.

Smashing Your Fears tackles your fear of failure at its root, encouraging you to act, and helping you to formulate the *why* behind your new proactive attitude.

Method

When filling in the table below, it is critical that you spend some time uncovering the real reasons for your procrastination or your need to be perfect.

Putting in a simple, yet shallow response, is not going to help you uncover the reasons you need to be perfect.

Answering thoughtfully, and ensuring you are really digging deep, will allow you to formulate meaningful actions, and a *why* that marries your purpose and your values.

Schedule a *Fearless-15* to get this exercise done, and complete this exercise for every task, or action you are avoiding or fearful of.

I have completed the first row of this table as an example for you.

Thought, feeling, or avoidance technique you are using as an excuse not to get things done.	Things I do that perpetuate my *suffering* when I think, feel, or act this way.	Action that will facilitate *joy, happiness, and vitality* in my life.
I am not artistic, and anything I paint is ugly. I am avoiding my *Fail for the Bigger Picture* exercise because it won't be perfect.	I am avoiding the very exercise that will help me embrace a growth mindset. Without this mindset, I will continue to be stuck in perfectionism.	I will do this exercise on Saturday morning. I have checked the weather forecast, purchased the products, and am committed to having fun while I grow to accept myself.

Blinker Removal: Seeing the Problem for What It Is

Having a perfectionist attitude and getting caught up in perfectionism can make us believe that our problems are a lot bigger than they really are.

The great thing about beliefs is that they're merely perceptions that have formed a set of ideas or thoughts in our minds, and we can change our thoughts.

You may have gone your whole life believing one thing to be true, but, when presented with evidence, you can change your mind and your beliefs.

Seeing a problem for what it actually is can help you make a decision and act quickly on that decision because it removes fear from the equation.

Think about it this way: When you were younger, and you feared the monster under your bed, shining a light into the dark void dispelled that fear.

Seeing the Problem for What It Is illuminates the dark void where your fears reside and shows you the real reason you are fearful so that you can dispel these fears.

Method

The goal of this exercise is to help you uncover your fears, automatic negative thoughts, and actions that are causing you to struggle.

It's important that you uncover your problematic thoughts as well as your behaviors or actions that prove those thoughts are right.

As such, you're going to need to be mindful and put some thought into where your fears and behaviors originate from.

Simply saying, "I am procrastinating," isn't going to cut it.

Fill in the table below so that you can uncover not only your thoughts but also your behaviors, and then set actionable goals to overcome your learned behaviors.

Negative thoughts or feelings you are experiencing.	Behaviors that reinforce these thoughts or behaviors.	How to overcome negative behaviors.	How do this goal tie into my values and new beliefs?
I think I am incapable of getting fit because I am uncoordinated.	I find any excuse not to exercise, blaming the weather, my health, and everything in between.	Set a *Fearless-15* every second day to exercise. Start by walking for 15 minutes.	I believe my body needs to be healthy for my mind to be healthy. Becoming fit helps my body and my mind.

Mistakes and failure are a part of life, and without making mistakes, you would never have learned half the skills you have today.

Methodically practicing skills, embracing failure as a part of the learning process, and uncovering the reasons you fear failure are important to overcoming perfectionism.

You cannot be perfect… And that is perfectly okay!

As long as you are learning from your mistakes, creating goals that fall in line with your values, and adding a sprinkle of humor to your failure faux pas, fear cannot take over your every thought and action.

CHAPTER 6:

Managing Perfectionism Stress

It can be tempting to view your perfectionism as a strength, and it can be, if you learn to manage it properly, but when being perfect cripples your ability to finish a task, or even get it started, being perfect is anything but strong.

You see, your strength lies in your perfectionist tendencies, but your strength is not perfectionism… Confusing, I know!

Brené Brown, an American professor in social work, once said, "When perfectionism is driving us, shame is riding shotgun, and fear is that annoying backseat driver!"

This statement couldn't be more true, especially when you realize just how many life experiences you have missed out on because of your perfectionism.

When perfectionism is properly managed, it allows us to manage stress, harnessing it for its actual purpose.

You see, stress is not fear, nor is it shame; it's a physiological process that allows us to perform at our optimum for short periods of time.

We are not meant to live in a perpetual state of stress. Instead, we're meant to acknowledge our stress so that we can use it to our advantage.

The adult brain is remarkable when it comes to stress, and its structure as well as its functional plasticity give all of us the ability to respond properly to stressful experiences if we choose to manage our stress.

Wiring Your Brain for Stress?

Plasticity is our brain's ability to adapt to changes and learn new information through the formation of neural pathways.

As you know, for many years, it was thought the brain stopped learning and developing after adolescence, which is simply not true.

When it comes to stress, choosing to avoid stress, or learning poor coping techniques, like perfectionism, can lead to the incorrect neural placement and our synapses firing incorrectly.

All of this can lead to cognitive distortions forming – "I can't do this because I am a failure" – an inability to make decisions, persistent anxiety, and the inability to regulate our emotions.

The issue with the above side effects of not managing stress is that we begin to express our stress outward, which is just another way of saying our behaviors begin to change… and not for the *good* either.

In addition, an imbalance in the brain begins to take its toll on our bodies as well, messing with our immune system, metabolism, muscles, circulatory system, and even our pain tolerance.

Managing stress, and learning to use your perfectionist tendencies to get things done, rather than being governed by the stress that is caused by your perfectionism, is the way to go. (McEwen, 2017).

Insisting on being perfect, or completing tasks to perfection does more harm than good, to your mental and physical health, period.

Ultimately, perfectionism leads to your self-esteem being knocked out, your relationships falling apart, and your health following suit very quickly.

I'm the prime example of how quickly burnout can set in when perfectionism reigns supreme!

It really is no surprise *why* perfectionism is on the rise. You just need to log into any social media account and view the airbrushed people living impossibly lavish lifestyles, and filling their schedules with one appearance, business, and task after the next to understand it.

But social media isn't real, and most, if not all, of those people have an army of other people they delegate to. The remainder of them either suffer from burnout themselves, or, at some point, will admit they shoved the chaos of their lives out of frame while filming.

Of course, there are certain instances where being perfect is a necessity... I mean, I'm not sure I'd want a surgeon with a "fail fast, learn fast" attitude operating on me, or a pilot landing my plane with the same view on life.

Having said that, these people, of whom perfection is demanded, practiced, studied, and learned for a considerable amount of time, and guess what?

They failed time and time again in a safe environment so that they could learn not to fail when it counts.

The reality for most of us is that our imperfections and our mistakes carry tiny consequences, and 99.9% of the time, good enough is, well, good enough!

I'm a Leaf on a Stream: An Exercise in Acceptance

Stress can get the better of us, and some people are so accustomed to feeling stressed that they don't even realize how profoundly they are affected by the stress they are carrying around with them.

Years ago, before my burnout, I remembered chatting with a friend who asked me mid-conversation why I was tensing and rolling my shoulders.

When I explained I had been battling through muscle aches and pains for a couple of weeks with no explanation, he looked at me with a nod and said, "Stress, man, it's a killer."

I brushed this statement off, and looking back now; I realize that I was perpetually stressed.

My job, my perfectionism, my inability to complete a task, self-inflicted unreasonable deadlines, critical thoughts, an unwillingness to take care of my body or my mind... All of these things were adding up, and I had become completely desensitized to the warning signs my body was giving me.

Mindfulness practices are a great way to get back in touch with our body and our mind, of course, and help us identify stress we may be carrying as well as let that stress go in a healthy way.

You will, of course, need to find other ways to combat your stress – like getting things done before the last minute and silencing your inner critic – but you need to manage the stress you are feeling in the meantime.

In fact, some, or even all, of the exercises in this book may cause you some stress in the initial phases as you step outside of your comfort zone and begin to reclaim your life.

While mindfulness comes in a lot of different forms you can try and practice, incorporating visualization and meditation with it at least once a day is a great way to help alleviate stress.

Method

The *Leaf on a Stream* exercise is designed to incorporate mindfulness, meditation, and visualization to help identify stress, calm your mind, and release the tension you are feeling.

Schedule five minutes to do this exercise, or do it before you go to sleep at night to help induce great quality sleep.

1. Find a comfortable space to lie down.

2. Place your hands at your sides or on your chest, and breathe deeply.

3. Inhale through your nose, and exhale through your mouth.

4. Close your eyes.

5. Notice your breath as you breathe.

6. If a thought enters your mind, imagine a leaf.

7. Now, place that thought on the leaf, and imagine it floating away.

8. Return your focus to your breathing.

9. Allow your mind to enter a beautiful forest.

10. As you walk through this forest, take in all of the sights, sounds, and smells.

11. You can hear a river in the distance…

12. Imagine you are walking through the forest. How does it feel? What do you hear, smell, and see? Is there anything you can touch?

13. As you reach the river, refocus on your breath.

14. Inhale through your nose and exhale through your mouth.

15. Take a step into the river.

16. Feel the cool water envelop your skin as you get deeper and deeper.

17. Imagine you are floating on your back, like a leaf on a calm river – weightless as the water cleanses you.

18. Focus on the sky above you and breathe…

Should you be doing this exercise during the day and you do not want to fall asleep, make sure to set a timer with an alarm.

Uncovering Stress: From Stress Ball to Stress Mastery

When you are on stress auto-pilot, or you're feeling really stressed, it can be difficult to identify what exactly is triggering your stress and why it is occurring.

I hear you screaming, "It's my perfectionism that's causing my stress!" And, yes, this is the obvious answer, but what is causing your perfectionism?

To move from *Stress Ball to Stress Mastery*, you need to become a master at identifying the root cause of your stress.

A lot of your perfectionism will be based on a series of belief systems that have developed over the years, but these beliefs were founded on… You guessed it… Stress!

Uncovering the reasons for your stress isn't enough, though, and you will need to explore ways that help to alleviate your stress.

Whether this is 10 minutes of pounding the sidewalk during a brisk run, reading a book, or, dare I say it, painting your boundary wall, stress alleviation is an integral part of learning to manage your stress.

When you were younger, things that stressed you out caused an emotional outburst that probably involved some form of movement, like throwing a tantrum, perhaps?

It turns out that the human body needs to rid itself of energy, and that energy includes nervous energy that is created by stress.

When completing this exercise, I'd like you to be mindful of this fact and look for ways that you can rid yourself of the energy of the stress you are experiencing.

Yes, mindfulness and meditation are great, and they are shown to help reduce stress levels astronomically, but you still need to physically or mentally move for the energy to be released.

Method

1. Print as many copies of the tables below as you need.

2. Make sure that you are being mindful when filling in the relevant categories, looking below the surface of the stressor.

3. Rate each of these stressors from 1 to 10, with 1 being the lowest level of stress you feel and 10 being the highest.

4. When filling in your stress reducers, make sure to think of ways you can reduce your stress every day which include some form of mental or physical movement.

5. Once you have filled in each relevant category, match your highest-rated stressor with your highest-rated stress protector.

Daily Stressors: What daily occurrences or tasks cause you to stress?

Stressor	1–10
1.	
2.	
3.	
4.	
5.	

What major events may have compounded these stressors: For example, you have received a warning for being tardy, and traffic now causes you anxiety.

Stressor	1–10
1.	
2.	
3.	
4.	
5.	

Life events that contribute to stressors include: For example, if you grew up in poverty, you may fear losing your job.

Stressor	1–10
1.	
2.	
3.	
4.	
5.	

Stress Reducers: Activities that can protect against and release stress.

Activities that make or made me happy: For example, spending time with your kids, eating a meal with friends, and so on.

Stressor	1–10
1.	
2.	
3.	
4.	
5.	

Healthy self-care activities that help me unwind: For example, journaling, painting, working out, yoga, and so on.

Stressor	1–10
1.	
2.	
3.	
4.	
5.	

External factors that could protect from stress: For example, financial stability, education, fitness, and so on.

Stressor	1–10
1.	
2.	
3.	
4.	
5.	

Mindfulness-Based Stress Reduction (MSBR): Mindful Hearing and/or Seeing

I know a lot of people push meditation and mindfulness aside, dismissing them as pseudoscience, but the fact remains that these two practices are some of the most effective psychological interventions around.

Mindfulness and meditation take practice, especially when you have a mind that is whirring with thoughts and an inner critic that drowns out all of your accomplishments.

Sometimes, the only thing holding you back from truly healing and letting go of your perfectionism once and for all is the one thing you are resisting or dismissing the most.

MSBR is a scientific, evidence-based form of therapy that helps to reduce anxiety, depression, stress, and even pain while seeking to eliminate the behaviors that are causing you stress in the first place.

Through mindfulness and taking action, MSBR techniques have been shown to significantly reduce anxiety and stress, giving a person the opportunity to focus their attention on changing behaviors (Goldin & Gross, 2010).

Mindful Hearing and/or Seeing is one of these MSBR techniques and is an incredibly effective grounding tool you can use when you feel like your stress is out of control.

Method

1. Find a place where you can sit uninterrupted, and that offers you a view of your surroundings. Be creative with your space – a window that can be opened, a balcony, porch, backyard, or even a park are great places to practice this exercise.

2. Without labeling the objects around you, start to take in the sights first and then the sounds.

3. Make sure you are not using a specific word to label an object. Instead of thinking "dog," focus on the color, texture, tone, and movement of the animal.

4. Close your eyes, and draw your focus to your breath. When you open your eyes, focus on something else.

5. Try to experience your environment in the same way a baby would… They know no labels, only sensory stimulation.

6. Make sure you are not passing judgment on what you are seeing and hearing. Instead, focus on the movements of whatever has drawn your attention.

7. Should you find your mind going back into its thoughts, or if you find yourself labeling or judging, shift your focus by looking at or hearing something new.

8. Sit in mindful listening and/or hearing for 10 minutes before returning your focus to your breath.

9. Inhale through your nose for a count of four and exhale for a count of four.

10. Repeat your breathing five times before continuing with your day.

Stress can cause chaos in your life and take its toll not only on your mental health but also on your physical health.

It's important that you learn to manage not only your stress but also take the time to uncover the reasons why you have a stress response.

A lot of the stress we feel is based on our own self-limiting beliefs and our perceptions of what is expected of us.

By letting go of these expectations, practicing acceptance, and becoming non-judgmental of ourselves, we can reduce our stress levels, building up our energy reserves to help us heal.

CHAPTER 7:

Making Sense of Thought Distortion – Escaping the Anxiety Whirlwind

Everyone, and I do mean every single person, experiences thought distortions at some point in their lives.

These thoughts could have been thinking you had done terribly in a test only to pass with an amazing grade or thinking you have made the worst possible decision and everything turned out great.

Thought distortions are your mind, or your thoughts leading you off course, making you believe an outcome is one thing when it probably is not.

And yes, out of an infinite number of possibilities, that one particular outcome could come to pass, but usually, it won't, or if you have the right mindset, it won't matter much.

What do I mean?

Well, the human brain is a marvelous creation. It steers the body toward an outcome based on our thoughts, which means if you're thinking the worst, you're going to see the worst, and probably end up manifesting it too.

That's right!

When you focus on the worst possible outcome, your brain will fixate on it and facilitate the outcome it thinks you want.

Ultimately, your brain tells your body what to do, but you can tell your brain what to do by changing your thought distortions and getting rid of your limiting beliefs.

In a sense, your thoughts, not your brain, sabotage your efforts, and you have control over what you do with your thoughts.

Let's say you were given a 3,000-piece puzzle. The picture on the box is something that interests you, and you would love to be able to complete the puzzle.

Your thoughts, however, are telling you, *"I'll never have enough time to do this! I'm so uncoordinated, I'll probably lose the pieces! With my luck, I'll get started, and something will happen to prevent me from finishing!"*

You fixate on these thoughts, ruminating about all of the things that could go wrong, and you avoid the puzzle for years on end because your mind will find distractions. Alternatively, you will unpack the puzzle with the notion that you're uncoordinated, drop a piece, and pack it up – your actions confirming your thoughts.

When we look at this scenario objectively, all it really takes to build the puzzle is to pick up one piece after the next and place it in the right space... Doesn't it?

Actually, building the puzzle takes very little thought.

You just *need* to build it!

But first, you need to work at identifying your thought distortions so that you can uncover what core beliefs are limiting your progress in life.

This all sounds incredibly easy, and once you have the knack for it, it probably will become easy, but at the beginning of your journey to shedding your distortions, you're going to need to be hypervigilant of your thoughts so that you can challenge them.

The reason for being vigilant is that thought distortions and cognitive distortions come in different forms, and they're usually buried very deeply in our root beliefs.

Just Build It!

Years ago, I watched an interview Oprah Winfrey conducted with Deepak Chopra.

In this interview, Chopra discusses the power of thought, and to demonstrate his point, he handed a small medallion on a string to Oprah.

He asked her to focus on the string, imagining that the medallion was still.

Next, he asked her to change her thinking to the medallion moving from left to right. She was to ensure that she wasn't moving her hand while holding the thought of this new movement in her mind.

The medallion, unbelievably, began moving from left to right.

This continued with different movements, much to the astonishment of Winfrey and the live audience.

Not convinced, I rummaged through my partner's trinkets until I found a suitable substitute.

Holding the necklace suspended in the air, I used every iota of my strength to hold the necklace still as my thoughts shifted through different movements.

Despite my best efforts to sabotage the experiment, the necklace, or at least my hand, obeyed my thoughts.

My cognitive distortion that this "made-for-TV-magic" was hogwash was completely destroyed, and I sat contemplating how many of my own distortions had prevented me from success.

I was a puppet... And my thoughts were the puppet master, and the real irony was that I could have taken control of my thoughts at any given time, but I chose not to.

For the perfectionist, there are some common forms of cognitive distortion that happen together or separately and that control our behaviors.

This doesn't mean you can't experience other forms, though.

The most common form of thought distortion is polarized thinking, which leads us to believe the world is black or white.

It's that "all or nothing" attitude we have that leads us to create unrealistic standards for ourselves and sometimes for others.

So limiting is this distortion, that our motivation to try just about anything is affected because, subconsciously, we know that we are setting ourselves up for failure.

Black-or-white thinking often drives us to blame as well, and we end up catastrophizing outcomes, believing that the worst will happen, even if, on some level, we know how highly improbable this outcome is.

When we catastrophize, we get stuck in a loop of *what-ifs*, *shoulds*, and *coulds*. We become so convinced of any disastrous outcome that we dismiss the facts. We guard ourselves with a set of ironclad rules to help avoid ever having to deal with all of these made-up scenarios.

I should.

I could.

I would.

These are all meaningless statements because *none* of them lead to action, and the only use they have is making us sound like the beginnings of the next Dr. Seuss bestseller.

Discovering Me: Removing Limiting Core Beliefs

Your core beliefs are the perceptions that you have formed about yourself, other people, and the world.

The issue with any belief that we hold is that unless we challenge it or seek to understand why we believe in the things we do, our very beliefs can hold us hostage.

The great thing about beliefs is that they can be challenged because they're not facts, and 99.9% of the time, beliefs are just not true.

When we hold onto our beliefs and live our lives in accordance with the self-limiting beliefs we have, it affects our behaviors, our mental health, and our ability to make decisions.

And, because your behavior is directly affected by your beliefs, you begin to look for evidence that what you believe is the absolute truth.

You have to get into the habit of uncovering your own self-limiting beliefs, challenging them, and reframing them into something that facilitates positive action so that you can overcome your perfectionism.

Method

Removing Limiting Core Beliefs is an exercise you can do as many times as you like to help you uncover your self-limiting beliefs.

When completing the first statements below, it is important that you don't take too much time to think about the answers.

The reason for this is that your self-limiting beliefs are instinctive, which means they are usually the first answer that pops into your head.

The thoughts you have after your instinctive answer are usually the internal argument that validates or disputes your initial thought.

Limiting Belief

I am...	
The world is...	
Other people are...	

Analysis

After completing the statements above, you can now take the time to think about what you have written.

Ask yourself

1. How do these statements make me feel?

2. When is the first time you remember having this opinion?

3. What do you think created these beliefs – was there a specific event or behavior?

4. Does anyone in your life hold the same beliefs?

Challenge

Think about your original statements and ask yourself:

1. Do these beliefs serve a purpose?

2. Do these beliefs help or hinder me?

Now complete the statements below, reframing each of them as a belief that would improve your life and your well-being.

I am...	
The world is...	
Other people are...	

Reframe

Looking at the reframed beliefs above, answer the following questions:

1. How can you use these new beliefs to help you overcome your perfectionism?

2. How do these new beliefs help you interpret the world and your circumstances differently?

3. How can your new beliefs help you achieve success?

Cataloging Inner Rules: Keep It or Trash It

Everyone has a set of inner rules that are linked to their thoughts and beliefs.

These inner rules dictate your behaviors and your reasoning when making a decision.

While you may not be able to identify or verbalize these rules because they're so deeply ingrained in your subconscious, they do exist. These inner rules are usually the reasoning or justification you will use when you are making just about any decision.

Some of these rules are, of course, great and help you make good decisions, but others are maladaptive.

An example of this for perfectionists are maladaptive rules that can make you think that making mistakes somehow makes you a terrible person.

I remember watching a kid's movie, The Croods, years ago.

In this movie, a cave-dwelling family lived by the rule that anything different or outside of the familiar was bad.

I won't give away the entire plot line, but by challenging this rule, the world opened up for the family.

Challenging your inner rules is as important as challenging your self-limiting beliefs because both of these are interlinked and directly influence your behaviors.

Method

Fill in the form below.

Make sure that you are using this exercise for every maladaptive inner rule you identify.

Answer the questions below, and then fill in the relevant tables.

1. What maladaptive rule have you identified?
2. Did you break this maladaptive rule?
3. If you did break the rule, what feelings did you have?

Pros and Cons of Your Rule

Pros: How can this rule help you?	**Cons**: How can this rule hurt you?

Keep the Rule	**Modify the Rule**	**Trash the Rule**

Rewrite your rule below and print it so that you can be reminded of this rule whenever you default to maladaptive behavior.

My new rule is...

The Cost: What Would I Do?

In the business world, companies do a cost-benefit analysis to determine whether the rules, regulations, and decisions an organization is making are worthwhile.

The reason cost-benefit analysis is so useful is that it allows you to set your emotions aside and look at an issue through unbiased eyes.

Remember how I told you that not all decisions are big ones?

Well, some decisions are pretty life-altering, and even if you are making smaller decisions like a pro, having to make a large decision can throw you back into analysis paralysis and old perfectionist habits.

A good solution to this problem is for you to perform a cost-benefit analysis of your life to simplify your decision-making processes.

Method

Schedule a *Fearless-15* so that you can thoughtfully, and without bias, fill in the worksheet below.

Make sure that you are setting your emotions aside so that you can evaluate your choice as if it were a business decision.

Question	Answer
What decision do I need to make?	
How will this decision affect my life?	
What would the payoff/benefit of this decision be?	
What would be the cost of this decision?	
What would the future look like if I decided to act?	

What would the future look like if I decided not to act?	
If I visualize the future after making this decision, what do I feel?	
My commitment when it comes to this decision is...	

Thought distortions, self-limiting beliefs, and the inner rules we all create for ourselves can have a profound impact on our behaviors and our ability to make decisions and act.

By challenging your inner thoughts, uncovering your self-limiting beliefs, and creating new inner rules, you can find out exactly what it is that is holding you back in life. And, once you know what is holding you back, you can become unstuck so that you can move forward and create new rules that facilitate positive growth.

Always remember, beliefs are changeable; they adapt and evolve, and if you are prepared to challenge the negative beliefs you have, replacing them with beliefs that encourage a growth mentality, you can better manage your stress, your anxiety, and your life as a whole.

CHAPTER 8:

Be Your Own Superhero – Unlocking Inner Joy and Happiness

In case you hadn't noticed… Perfectionism takes a lot of mental energy, and I do mean a *lot*!

We are so busy making sure we are perfect, that others are perfect, or debating all of the reasons we should or shouldn't get things done that we become blissfully unaware of the burnout that is happening inside of us.

And it's not that we don't feel burnout creeping in, either. We're reminded of our exhaustion almost every single day, and as night creeps in and we think we can finally rest, our inner critic wakes up to remind us of the failure we think we are. But we push aside these nagging feelings, telling ourselves that we should do better… Be better.

We rinse and repeat this cycle of pure exhaustion over and over again, and sometimes we feel like there isn't even an iota of mental energy left to give ourselves.

Simply put, we forget to show up for ourselves, and we push aside the fact that our mental and physical health matter.

In the throes of perfectionism, we begin to make excuses for how we are feeling, brushing off our anxiety, stress, and exhaustion as yet another reason we are not good enough.

We lie awake at night, ruminating thoughts keeping us awake, hoping that someone will save us from ourselves.

We berate ourselves for our own flaws without ever thinking about the fact that our flaws are the building blocks with which we build ourselves on our individual paths to success.

And we want to be saved… really do, but we fail to see that the only person capable of saving us, is ourselves.

Here You Come To Save the Day

I'm not taking anything away from you, or the frustration you are feeling, but the most important aspect of becoming your own superhero is to realize that everyone has stuff they're dealing with.

The world is a chaotic, sometimes maddening place, and when we get lost in the details of this chaos, or try to keep up with it, it can leave us feeling like we are drowning.

Now, remember I said everyone is dealing with stuff?

They cannot save you because they're busy keeping themselves afloat!

When we're struggling emotionally and being pulled down by the weight of our perfectionism, it can sometimes feel better to avoid absolutely everything.

You may tell yourself that you're simply not strong enough to deal with this, that you're too tired, or that someone will save you before you are completely engulfed by this torrent that is perfectionism.

And, as you tread water, you will slowly realize that your life is falling apart, and at some point, it hits you… No one is coming to save you!

If you're reading this book and completing the exercises within it, then you have already become acutely aware of the fact that you need to save yourself, and for that, I applaud you.

If you're not sure whether or not you have the strength to save yourself, let me be the first to don my cheerleading outfit so that I can cheer you into superhero status.

And, if you're not even sure whether your perfectionism is that bad, it's time to go through the checklist below. If most of the items on this checklist don't yet apply to you, you're in the perfect – notice what I did there – position to nip your perfectionism in the bud before it consumes you.

- If you've forgotten, you have a choice, and that you need to act on your choice, your perfectionism has the better of you.

- If you're more concerned with what you should be doing than what is the right thing for you to be doing, perfectionism is taking over.

- If you're ruminating over past failures or fretting about future failures, you're drowning in your perfectionism.

- If every decision, problem, or obstacle provokes an emotional reaction in you, your perfectionism is driving you to burnout.

- Finally, if you have lost yourself, your passions, and your purpose, and you feel like the only way anyone will accept you is if you are perfect, your perfectionism has you in burnout.

But, it's never too late to rise from the ashes, and you do have the strength to save yourself, and the best part of it all is that you don't need to wear your underwear over tights, nor do you need a catchy name… Although the odd superhero pose never hurt anyone!

Backed by Science: The Superhero Pose Meditation!

I don't know many kids who haven't, at some point during their childhood, imagined, wished for, or pretended they were a superhero.

Every superhero comes with a couple of necessities, including an identifiable costume, their own superpower, and, of course, their signature superhero poses!

Being a superhero, or at the very least taking on those superhero necessities, doesn't need to stay in your childhood.

"Wait… What? I'm not going to don my underwear over my outwear to save the day!"

No, you don't need to hire a costume or fight bad guys undercover in the night, but these fictional superhero necessities didn't come about by chance.

You see, storytellers and creators, at least the good ones, are also keen observers of human behavior.

They know what people want from a hero and what a villain needs to be particularly disliked for, and they know how to have the hero overcome tragedy by using his or her superpowers and drawing strength from his or her posture.

Don't you believe me?

When you are getting ready for a date, an interview, or any important event, what do you instinctively do?

You get up, get clean, get dressed into your best clothes, and make sure your external appearance is agreeable or even unique so that you can make a lasting impression… your superhero costume!

When on your date, at the interview, or attending the event, you put your best foot forward, changing your body language and behavior to exude knowledge, awareness, and confidence, even if you're nervous or not feeling confident… your superpower and your superhero pose!

This may all sound absolutely ridiculous, but superhero posing is actually backed by science and has been shown to boost confidence, lower anxiety, and help you focus on the task at hand. In fact, superhero poses are practiced by successful business people, athletes, singers, actors, and motivational speakers the world over because it is so effective (Smit, 2021).

Method

The best time to practice your superhero pose is in the morning when you wake up or whenever you feel your confidence waning.

To start, add your superhero pose to your morning routine and practice it while your coffee or tea is brewing, or once you are dressed for the day.

If you're unsure of what a superhero pose looks like, start with the most basic of these poses, as described below.

If you want, you can search for pictures using the words "power pose" and "Wonder Woman."

1. Stand in front of a full-length mirror.

2. Close your eyes and take a deep breath, holding your inhale for a count of three and exhaling for a count of five.

3. Look at your body in the mirror, not your face.

4. Open your legs, shoulder-width apart.

5. Ball your hands into relaxed fists, and place your hands on your hips.

6. Puff out your chest and stand up straight, shoulders back.

7. Lift your chin slightly and fix your gaze on your face.

8. Stand in this pose for two minutes, concentrating on your posture.

9. Every time a thought enters your mind, focus on the part of body, adjusting your pose so that you are back in full superhero mode.

10. Don't forget to breathe and enjoy this moment of confidence!

Once your two minutes are up, take note of how your body and your mind feel… and then tell yourself, "I am my own superhero!"

Hero Analysis: I'm Not Rooting for the Anti-Hero

When writers are formulating the anti-hero or villain, they use a specific go-to formula to provoke negative emotions in the reader or viewer.

The villain will always have a strong connection to the hero, be motivated by things the hero doesn't agree with, and work against the hero, trying to ensure they never succeed.

Again, this anti-hero, or villain formula is not something that happened without thought, and writers follow these formulas because they know, on a psychological level, the story will be compelling.

The reason these stories get to us, and why we identify with the hero and abhor the villain in stories, is because storytelling is rooted in Jungian psychotherapy.

Now, I won't bore you with too many details, but it's important that you have some idea of who Carl Jung is, and why his form of psychotherapy is so critical to healing from your perfectionism.

Jung, through years of research, uncovered a pattern of inherited, universal thought patterns that occur within human beings. These thought patterns are instilled in us as a result of genetics, the lessons we learn as children, our upbringing, and what we think of ourselves as we move from adolescence into adulthood.

Carl Jung proved and denounced previous schools of thought that said human beings are born with a blank slate. He identified that we communicate with ourselves, others, and our environment from four states: the animus, the shadow, the persona, and the self.

Within each of these states, there are 12 archetypes, some with great traits and some with not-so-great traits.

So how does this all relate to the anti-hero in your life?

Well, you have a choice to nurture your positive archetype and silence your own villain.

That's right, every one of us has an inner hero but also a villain, working against our inner hero, trying to sabotage our efforts!

Method

You will need to schedule a *Fearless-15* to get this exercise done.

Make sure to be mindful and to silence your inner critic as you go through this worksheet so that you can uncover your inner hero and the villain that is sabotaging them.

The strengths listed for you are unconventional and are often not considered to be strengths at all when you are suffering from perfectionism.

You are NOT allowed to choose strengths outside of the supplied list, as it is important that you explore all of the things that make people strong and not just conventional ideas of strength.

If you cannot identify with any of the strengths listed, take a moment to be mindful and decide which of these strengths you want to possess.

Choose FIVE strengths from the following table:

Strengths List

Adventurous	Ambitious	Artistic	Assertive
Athletic	Aware	Brave	Confident
Cooperative	Creative	Curious	Disciplined
Empathetic	Enthusiastic	Fair	Flexible
Forgiving	Grateful	Honest	Humorous
Independent	Intelligent	Kind	Knowledgeable
Leader	Logical	Loving	Modest
Open-minded	Optimistic	Patient	Persistent
Self-controlled	Sensical	Spiritual	Wise

The Hero and the Anti-Hero: List your strengths below and identify the opposite quality.

I have provided an example in the first line of the table.

Hero/Strengths	Anti-Hero/Weaknesses
Example: Flexible	*Rigid*

Take a moment to reflect on the anti-hero column.

Which, if any, of these qualities are you perpetuating while stuck in perfectionism?

You DO NOT have to list all of them; ONLY the relevant ones.

My Weaknesses

My Superhero Powers Are...

The weaknesses you have identified have corresponding strengths, and because your anti-hero is working hard to sabotage your success, identifying your weaknesses is also a way to directly identify your own inner power.

For example, if you have identified yourself as being *rigid*, your superpower is actually *flexibility*, and working on this superpower will have you tap into your inner superhero!

Superhero Therapy: Real Hero Work for Healing

While superhero therapy is by no means a registered form of therapy, other evidence-based, registered forms of therapy, like CBT, DBT, and ACT, will sometimes use an element of superhero therapy.

Before beginning this final worksheet, you're going to need to spend some time thinking about heroes that resonate with you.

You don't need to be a traditional hero type of person either; you simply need to think back to books, films, or songs that featured a lead character who resonated with you.

Traditional superheroes always have a catalyst in their lives that drives them to change. For example, Spiderman, after experiencing a family loss as a result of crime, used his powers to rid his city of crime.

Buffy, the Vampire Slayer, worked through her inner pain so that she could learn to let go of control and accept who she was.

Even Han Solo from Star Wars overcame his egocentric ways to become self-sacrificing and humble.

Method

Answer the questions below.

1. Sit down with a journal or piece of paper.

2. Clear your mind of other thoughts, and draw your attention to stories or songs that have resonated with you.

3. Who was the hero in this story?

4. What was the catalyst that caused your hero pain or suffering?

5. What did your hero learn when on their journey to success?

6. What weaknesses do you identify with in your hero?

7. What strengths does your hero have that you would like?

8. If you had these strengths, how could you put them to use in the real world?

Here is an example of how you could answer the questions above.

I identify with Frodo Baggins. He had no control over his circumstances and was forced to do something he really didn't want to. Through his story, he learns to accept that he does not have to be a victim of his circumstances. He sets aside his victim mentality and chooses to be brave in the face of adversity so that he can save the world.

I am often fearful of change or working outside of my strengths. I want to gain control over my anxiety and fear so that I can be brave and step outside of my comfort zone.

In the real world, I could learn bravery in the face of adversity by volunteering or mentoring at a facility for disabled persons to learn everyday skills.

Superheroes are mystical, mythical, and the stuff legends are made of, but they're also based on people like you and me.

Becoming your own superhero is not as difficult as you think because every single person has both a villain and a hero inside of them.

By completing the exercises laid out in this chapter, identifying your own superpowers, and understanding what is driving your behavior, you can unlock your inner hero.

But it is up to you to act, to exact change, and to accept that the only way your anti-hero will ever stop sabotaging you is if you allow your hero to rise.

A Final Word on Calming Your Perfectionism Chaos

Perfectionism is debilitating, it's exhausting, and it's a whirlwind of chaos that we're constantly trying to get out of. But, it's also comforting because being stuck means we never have to face our fear of failure, make mistakes, or step outside of our comfort zone.

And all of this only adds to the whirlwind we're stuck in.

For most of us, perfectionism begins in our childhood once we become aware of others' opinions of us and begin to value what others think of us.

Once we begin to fear failure or making mistakes, our curiosity is squashed, and our inner critic begins to make itself heard.

We second-guess our decisions, procrastinate tasks out of fear, and convince ourselves that we *work best under pressure.*

All of this, of course, comes from a place that is rooted deeply in fear, and our emotions begin to govern our behaviors and our actions. Rather than embracing mistakes and failures as part of the learning process, we do everything in our power to avoid being anything but perfect.

I have met people who have recovered from perfectionism that has plagued them for years – who vividly remember tearing out pages and pages of their school notebooks because their hands were tired, and their writing was unacceptable.

I've spoken with people who live in hoarding squalor because they fear mistakenly throwing things away.

Perfectionism and its many masks can be soul-destroying, and when your inner critic finds affirmation in your behaviors, they present us with proof that we are all of the negative things we tell ourselves.

Overcoming perfectionism demands that you not only identify your perfectionism but also what is driving your perfectionist tendencies and why you are comfortable living in this fear.

It requires you to regain control over your anxiety so that you can release your inner child, explore your feelings with curiosity, and embrace mistakes as the essence of being a human being.

Because ultimately, life is practice… It is trial and error, rejection and acceptance, and a series of decisions we will have to make every single day of our existence.

Learning to take back your hijacked brain, permitting your mind to flow in the way it was designed to, and understanding that the bigger picture is just as beautiful when it contains flaws.

As you embark upon your journey to living a life that is perfectionism-free, I would like you to know that all things require action and energy.

Staying within your perfectionism requires as much, if not more, energy than stepping outside of it, and silencing your inner critic so that you can take action takes less energy than having to listen to the negativity it feeds you.

We live with the belief that perfectionism is the tool that saves us from drowning, and while that may be true to a certain extent, it is absolutely not the tool that teaches us to swim, either.

Perfectionism teaches us to tread water while we stare in exhaustion at the shore we could swim to.

And, no one can save you, nor should anyone save you, because you already know what to do; you just need to stop treading water and actually start to swim.

The biggest lesson I learned when recovering from my own perfectionism was a simple but difficult one… I had to surrender.

Surrender to my imperfections, surrender to the process, and surrender to my inner hero, who was begging to be let out.

I learned to laugh often, especially when I made mistakes, to forgive myself because I deserve to be treated with as much empathy as I treat others, and I set my mind free to be curious and messy without judgment.

Because here's the thing about life…

The only thing we will ever have control over is ourselves, and we can choose to allow ourselves to live in chaos, or we can choose to be happy in our flaws and free from the restraints of perfectionism.

References

Ackerman, C. (2017, January 18). *22 Mindfulness Exercises, Techniques & Activities For Adults (+ PDF's)*. Positive Psychology. https://positivepsychology.com/mindfulness-exercises-techniques-activities/

ACT Made Simple - Client Handouts and Worksheets. (Acceptance and Commitment Therapy.). (n.d.). Studylib. net. https://studylib.net/doc/25318825/act-made-simple---client-handouts-and-worksheets.---accep%E2%80%A6

Alderson-Day, B., & Fernyhough, C. (2015). Inner speech: Development, cognitive functions, phenomenology, and neurobiology. *Psychological Bulletin, 141*(5), 931–965. https://doi.org/10.1037/bul0000021

Cataloging Your Inner Rules. (n.d.-a). Positive Psychology. https://positive.b-cdn.net/wp-content/uploads/Cataloging-Your-Inner-Rules.pdf

Cherry, K. (2021, April 5). *The 6 Types of Basic Emotions and Their Effect on Human Behavior*. Verywell Mind. https://www.verywellmind.com/an-overview-of-the-types-of-emotions-4163976

Cognitive Restructuring Worksheet. (n.d.-b). Positive Psychology. https://positive.b-cdn.net/wp-content/uploads/2020/09/Cognitive-Restructuring-Worksheet.pdf

Core Beliefs Worksheet 1. (n.d.-c). Positive Psychology. https://positive.b-cdn.net/wp-content/uploads/Core-Beliefs-Worksheet-1.pdf

Extended Case Formulation Worksheet. (n.d.-d). Positive Psychology. https://positive.b-cdn.net/wp-content/uploads/2020/09/Extended-Case-Formulation-Worksheet.pdf

Foster Therapy. (2017, November 1). *Stop Procrastinating Now!* Foster Art and Wellness. https://fosterartandwellness.com/stop-procrastinating-now/

Genovese, D. J. (2018, September 20). *Deactivate your amygdala to combat procrastination*. Learning Fundamentals. https://learningfundamentals.com.au/deactivate-your-amygdala-to-combat-procrastination/

Goldin, P. R., & Gross, J. J. (2010). Effects of mindfulness-based stress reduction (MBSR) on emotion regulation in social anxiety disorder. *Emotion, 10*(1), 83–91. https://doi.org/10.1037/a0018441

James, M. (2016). *Limiting Beliefs* [PDF]. https://static1.squarespace.com/static/55d0282fe4b02b2904382a33/t/571c78e120c6472939a56427/1461483748116/Limiting+Beliefs+Fillable+Worksheet.pdf

Korman, K. (2020, July 16). *Paint Splatter Art the Easy Way: Techniques for Your Next Project*. Skillshare Blog. https://www.skillshare.com/en/blog/paint-splatter-art-the-easy-way-tips-and-tricks-for-your-next-project/

Langley Ph.D., T. (2014, May 14). *What Is Superhero Therapy? Psychology Today*. https://www.psychologytoday.com/us/blog/beyond-heroes-and-villains/201405/what-is-superhero-therapy#:~:text=For%20example%2C%20if%20someone%20wants

Leaves on a Stream mindfulness exercise. (n.d.-b). Therapist Aid. https://www.therapistaid.com/worksheets/leaves-on-a-stream-worksheet

Linden, D., Tops, M., & Bakker, A. B. (2020). Go with the flow: A neuroscientific view on being fully engaged. *European Journal of Neuroscience, 53*(4), 947-963. https://doi.org/10.1111/ejn.15014

Loscalzo, J. (2014). A Celebration of Failure. *Circulation, 129*(9), 953–955. https://doi.org/10.1161/circulationaha.114.009220

McEwen, B. S. (2017). Neurobiological and Systemic Effects of Chronic Stress. *Chronic Stress, 1*(1). https://doi.org/10.1177/2470547017692328

Newman, L. (2011, July 5). *5 Immediate and Easy Ways to Silence Your Inner Critic*. Tiny Buddha. https://tinybuddha.com/blog/5-immediate-and-easy-ways-to-silence-your-inner-critic/

Phil Gowler. (2018, March 20). *The Parent-Adult-Child model. Simple yet it works!* Phil Gowler. https://www.philgowler.co.uk/therapies/the-parent-adult-child-model-simple-yet-it-works/

Pignatiello, G. A., Martin, R. J., & Hickman, R. L. (2018). Decision fatigue: A conceptual analysis. *Journal of Health Psychology, 25*(1). https://doi.org/10.1177/1359105318763510

Racine, N. M., Pillai Riddell, R. R., Khan, M., Calic, M., Taddio, A., & Tablon, P. (2015). Systematic Review: Predisposing, Precipitating, Perpetuating, and Present Factors Predicting Anticipatory Distress to Painful Medical Procedures in Children. *Journal of Pediatric Psychology, 41*(2), 159–181. https://doi.org/10.1093/jpepsy/jsv076

Reward Replacement Worksheet. (n.d.-e). Positive Psychology. https://positive.b-cdn.net/wp-content/uploads/Reward-Replacement-Worksheet.pdf

Rieman, A. (n.d.). *The Power of The Superhero Project*. The Superhero Project. https://static1.squarespace.com/static/5e83b4febd8ad96a2b4ef0f6/t/5f19dd16e439317cfebdc84f/1595530518521/Ali+Strong+placard.pdf

Robbins, M. (2017). *Mel Robbins → The 5 Second Rule*. Mel Robbins. https://www.melrobbins.com/5secondrule

Schroeder, K., Durrleman, S., Çokal, D., Sanfeliu Delgado, A., Masana Marin, A., & Hinzen, W. (2021). Relations between intensionality, theory of mind and complex syntax in autism spectrum conditions and typical development. *Cognitive Development, 59*. https://doi.org/10.1016/j.cogdev.2021.101071

Smit, M. (2021, May 31). *Superhero Pose: The Benefits Of Power Posing*. Thrive Global. https://community.thriveglobal.com/superhero-pose-the-benefits-of-power-posing/#:~:text=So%2C%20how%20to%20stand%20in

Stress Exploration Daily Hassles. (n.d.-c). Therapist Aid. https://www.therapistaid.com/worksheets/stress-exploration

Therapist Aid. (n.d.-a). G*etting Rid of ANTS: Automatic Negative Thoughts Worksheet*. Positive Psychology. https://positive.b-cdn.net/wp-content/uploads/Getting-Rid-of-ANTS-Automatic-Negative-Thoughts.pdf

Urge Surfing. (n.d.-d). Therapist Aid. https://Www.therapistaid.com/Worksheets/Urge-Surfing-Handout; Therapist Aid.

Values and Problems. (n.d.-f). Positive Psychology. https://positive.b-cdn.net/wp-content/uploads/2019/06/Values-and-Problems.pdf

Weiler, J. (2018, August 22). *How brains of doers differ from those of procrastinators*. News.rub.de. https://news.rub.de/english/press-releases/2018-08-22-neuroscience-how-brains-doers-differ-those-procrastinators

Printed in Great Britain
by Amazon

27589935R00057